Tell Me Why

WHY?

Leaves Change Color

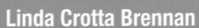

Linda Crotta Brennan

Published in the United States of America by Cherry Lake Publishing
Ann Arbor, Michigan
www.cherrylakepublishing.com

Content Adviser: Dr. Stephen S. Ditchkoff, Professor of Wildlife Sciences,
Auburn University, Auburn, Alabama
Reading Adviser: Marla Conn, ReadAbility, Inc.

Photo Credits: TK

Library of Congress Cataloging-in-Publication Data

Brennan, Linda Crotta, author.
 Leaves change color / by Linda Crotta Brennan.
    pages cm. -- (Tell me why)
 Summary: "Offers answers to the most compelling questions about the
changing seasons. Age-appropriate explanations and appealing photos.
Additional text features and search tools, including a glossary and an
index, help students locate information and learn new words."-- Provided by
publisher.
 Audience: K to grade 3.
 Includes bibliographical references and index.
 ISBN 978-1-63188-008-7 (hardcover) -- ISBN 978-1-63188-051-3 (pbk.) --
ISBN 978-1-63188-094-0 (pdf) -- ISBN 978-1-63188-137-4 (ebook) 1.
Leaves--Color--Juvenile literature. 2. Fall foliage--Juvenile literature.
3. Autumn--Juvenile literature. 4. Seasons--Juvenile literature. I.
Title.

QK649.B74 2015
581.4'8--dc23
                                2014005711

Cherry Lake Publishing would like to acknowledge the work of The Partnership for 21st Century Skills.
Please visit *www.p21.org* for more information.

Printed in the United States of America
Corporate Graphics Inc.

Table of Contents

So Many Colors 4

Food for Trees 8

Winter Weather 12

Two Kinds of Trees 18

Think About It 22

Glossary 23

Find Out More 23

Index 24

About the Author 24

So Many Colors

Ana laughed and ran through the pile of fallen leaves. They flew up and were blown around by the wind.

She picked up a pointy red-and-yellow leaf. "This one is pretty," she said.

Ana's grandmother, her tata, smiled. "It will be lovely on our place mats."

Ana found a gold-colored one. "This one is like a little goldfish."

Tata spread her arms. "The leaves are so beautiful. I grew up in Cuba. The leaves

LOOK!

Have you seen leaves like this where you live? Were they on trees or on the ground? What season was it?

Collecting leaves is one way to learn about them.

5

didn't change color there. Our weather was usually warm."

"Why do leaves change color?" asked Ana.

Tata knew the answer. In places with warm summers and cold winters, leaves change color in the fall. Green leaves turn red, orange, and yellow.

The leaves of different kinds of trees turn different colors. Birch leaves turn yellow. Oak leaves turn red-brown. Maple leaves turn orange, yellow, and red.

In an area with many trees, leaves might completely cover the ground.

Food for Trees

Ana placed the gold leaf on her piece of poster board. She put the red-and-yellow leaf next to it. She ran her finger along its pointy edges. They still had a little green. "What makes all the leaf colors, Tata?"

"The colors are from special chemicals called **pigments**." Tata pointed to the leaf's green edges. "In spring and summer, leaves have lots of green pigment. They have some orange and yellow pigments, too. But you can't see them because of all the green."

These maple leaves have a little bit of green pigment left.

The green pigment is called **chlorophyll**. It has a special job. **Photosynthesis** happens when chlorophyll turns sunlight into sugar and starch. The sugar and starch is food for the tree.

Orange and yellow pigments help gather sunlight for the tree's food. These pigments are called **carotenoids**.

"What about the red colors?" asked Ana.

"Those are different," said Tata. "They aren't made until the fall."

Light
Energy

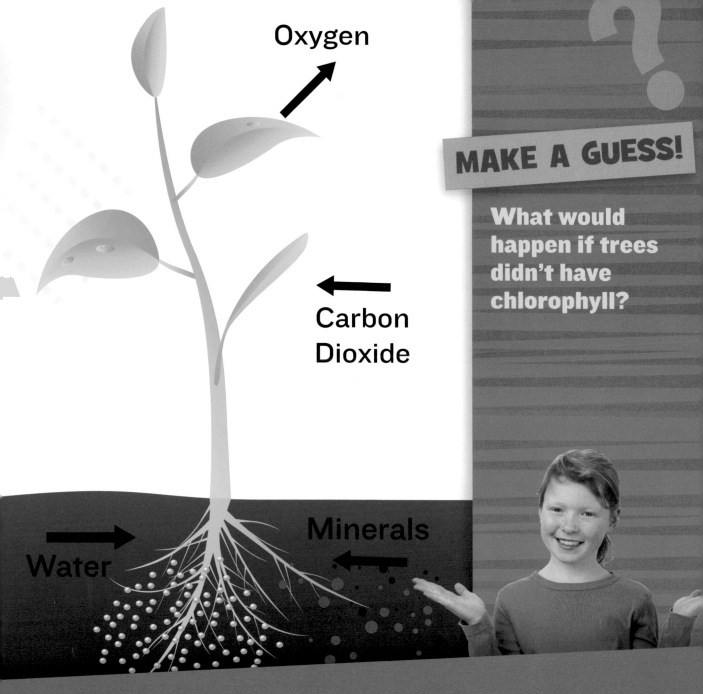

Oxygen

Carbon Dioxide

Water

Minerals

This is how photosynthesis happens.

MAKE A GUESS!

What would happen if trees didn't have chlorophyll?

Winter Weather

Ana's leaf place mat looked just right. She taped the leaves down. "But why do leaves change color in the fall?"

Tata handed Ana another piece of tape. "In the fall, the days get shorter," said Tata. "The trees prepare for winter. They stop making chlorophyll. With the green pigment gone, the red and yellow colors show through."

"What about the red?" asked Ana.

What if leaves never changed color? What if they stayed on the trees in winter?

This is how leaves look in the summertime with green pigment.

13

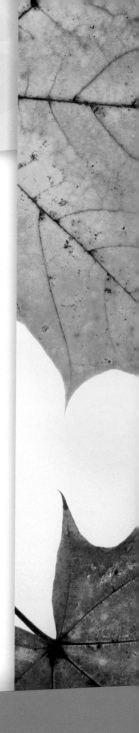

Tata picked up a leaf and pointed to the end of its stem. "Before leaves fall, scars form at their base. Sometimes the scars trap sugars in the leaves. The trapped sugars change into red pigments."

Ana smiled and patted the pile of leaves she had collected. "So all these beautiful leaves are from yellow, orange, and red pigments."

Sugars can get trapped in leaves before they fall.

"Leaves don't change color when it is warm all the time in winter. When the leaves don't change color, they don't fall off the trees. Near the **equator**, it doesn't get cold in winter. The trees don't lose their leaves."

In **temperate zones**, leaves change color in the fall. These are places with warm summers and cold winters.

The leaves on these trees will continue to fall through the winter months.

Two Kinds of Trees

Ana looked out the window. "The pine trees are still green."

"They don't have broad leaves. They have needles instead," said Tata. "These needles will stay on the trees in winter. They don't change color."

There are two kinds of trees, **deciduous** and **coniferous**. Deciduous trees have broad leaves. Coniferous trees have needles.

Most coniferous trees stay green in the fall. But, the needles on some coniferous trees change from green to yellow or brown in the winter and drop off.

Broad leaves are fragile. Their thin tissues would freeze in winter. So the tree must lose its leaves. Needles are tough. They have a heavy wax coating. It protects the needles from freezing. So needles usually stay on the tree in winter.

Outside, the wind blew more leaves off the trees.

"Look at them. They are so pretty," said Ana. "I wish we could use all of them for our place mats!"

Too many leaves on the ground can harm the grass.

Think About It

What else would you like to know about trees and their leaves? Write down at least three questions. Then go online with an adult or go to your local library to find answers!

Using information from Web sites or other books, make two lists. One list should describe deciduous trees. The other should describe coniferous trees. Compare the similarities and differences between the two kinds of trees.

Glossary

carotenoids (kuh-RAH-teh-noidz) orange and yellow plant pigments

chlorophyll (KLOR-uh-fil) a green pigment in plants that changes sunlight into sugar and starch

coniferous (kuh-NIF-ur-uhs) trees with cones and needles

deciduous (dih-SIH-joo-uhs) trees with broad leaves

equator (i-KWAY-tur) an imaginary line around the center of the earth

photosynthesis (foh-toh-SIN-thi-sis) a process that plants and trees go through as they make their food

pigments (PIG-muhnts) chemicals that create colors

temperate zones (TEM-pur-it ZOHNZ) the areas of moderate temperatures between the hot tropic zone and the cold zones near the North and South Poles

Find Out More

Books:

Felix, Rebecca. *What Happens to Leaves in Fall?* Ann Arbor, MI: Cherry Lake Publishing, 2013.

Hicks, Terry Allan. *Why Do Leaves Change Color?* New York: Marshall Cavendish, 2011.

Owen, Ruth. *Science and Craft Projects with Trees and Leaves.* New York: PowerKids Press, 2013.

Web Sites:

EcoKids—Types of Trees
www.ecokids.ca/pub/eco_info/topics/forests/types_of_trees.cfm
This Web site gives details about the difference between coniferous and deciduous trees.

Environmental Education for Kids—Why Do Leaves Change Color?
http://dnr.wi.gov/eek/veg/trees/treestruecolor.htm
Learn more about using leaf color to help you identify different kinds of trees.

Highlights Kids—Science Questions: How and Why Do Leaves Fall off Trees?
www.highlightskids.com/science-questions/how-and-why-do-leaves-fall-trees
Read more about leaves and how trees prepare for winter.

Index

broad leaves, 18

carotenoids, 10
chlorophyll, 10, 11, 12
colors, 4–7, 8, 10, 12, 14
coniferous trees, 18, 19

deciduous trees, 18

equator, 16

fall, 6, 16, 19
food, 8–11

needles, 18,19, 20

photosynthesis, 10, 11
pigments, 8, 9, 12, 13, 14
pine trees, 18

starch, 10
sugars, 10, 14, 15
summer, 6, 13, 16
sunlight, 10

temperate zones, 16
trees, 6, 9, 18–20

winter, 6, 12–17, 20

About the Author

Linda Crotta Brennan has a master's degree in education. She spent her life around books, teaching, and working at the library. Now she's a full time writer who loves learning new things. She lives with her husband and golden retriever. She has three grown daughters and a growing gaggle of grandchildren.